the garden of eye candy

the garden of eye candy

he fashioning and creation of characters and dolls have existed from the beginning of human civilization. In the past, it was carved into the walls of caves, or
made into dolls using raw materials found in nature. Human kind have always
known a fascination, if not a need, in producing other beings in our likeness,
much like the creation stories of how God fashioned us in 'his/her' own image.

These toys evolved into a fine craft with time, and were given to us as children. As our
playthings and friends, they became an integral part of our imaginations and psyches.
They served as markers and witnesses in our personal histories, appearing as characters
in our stories, and as such, began a life of their own, out of the hands of their creators,
in a world of their own.

Toy culture and these iconic images and characters, have grown in our time to be a huge
phenomenon. It crosses the boundaries of fine art, high and low culture, the sweet and
sometimes dark aspects ourselves. The Japanese were at the forefront with their cutting
edge productions of Anime and Manga, prompting an Otaku cult which today has spread
all over the world. US animation productions, from Mickey Mouse to the Simpsons have
become household names and larger than life characters in our daily lives.

We are lucky to have now, characters, icons, toys to love well into adult hood. From the
whimsical to adorable, erotic to innocent to the dark and gothic, luring us into their lush
worlds, of fairy tales, dreams and inspiration, where id driven impulses and alter egos
come to life. We invite you to slip into this mysterious parallel world of the imagination
with us in the Garden of Eye Candy.

Contents

You must have an imagination in order to react to imagery, otherwise it would just be forms and colors and mean nothing. Art is like a powerful drug that stimulates imagination.

Amy Sol is based in Las Vegas, Nevada, living in close proximity to the desert. She describes her living environment as quiet and simple, a perfect environment for daydreaming and creating. Amy cites the reason as to why she has remained settled in Las Vegas, her nuclear family has put down roots there, and she likes to be near them.

The paintings of Amy are born out of a dreamy and vast imagination. They have been described by fans of her work as whimsical, surreal and fantasy like. A sense of peace is conveyed through her artwork, making her pieces highly sought after. Her subject matter are alluring girls and exotic plant life, teeming with muted colors akin to the hues of the desert. Swirling and pale ochre, burnt yellows and oranges are part of her unique palette of colors.

Examining her influences, Amy reveals a life long interest in nature. This obsession has seen Amy seeking out imagery in the form of biological drawings of plants and animals in picture books and encyclopedias as a child. Her obsession shines through in her meticulous, detailed depiction of plants and creatures.

She says, "the characters and settings are part of a story that my subconscious is making an effort to tell. The colors and forms are the tone of my voice. I am the narrator."

The journey that she has taken to become a successful artist was not an altogether easy one. Before Amy was able to make a living off her art, she says that she has worked almost every imaginable odd job. Though she has never been classically trained as an artist, her skill attests to her dedication towards her art. Of art school, she muses, "I appreciate and respect school and conventional learning

with one side of my brain. The other side wants to be exorcized by my free uneducated will."

Working with the medium of acrylic on wood, Amy painstakingly layers her paintings, working with large areas of flat color. She is what you would call an 'intuitive artist', similar to the folk art vein, as instead of planning her paintings beforehand, she allows her imagination to unfold and guide the process and imagery. While trying to shed light on her drive to create, Amy relates to Carl Jung, the Swiss psychiatrist and his principles of creativity. He emphasized the importance of dreams, art and mythology when trying to understand the human psyche.

Amy believes that it is not a need for connection that humans have with characters but instead, an experience that a person may have with an image creates the attraction. "I often hear people say that an image spoke to them,

I've heard people say "it speaks to me" or "it makes me feel". I've felt that feeling before when looking at artwork. I think that connection-feeling is imagination itself at work on the observer. Logic and science cannot satisfactorily explain it to me otherwise. You must have an imagination in order to react to imagery; otherwise it would just be forms and colors and mean nothing. Art is like a powerful drug that stimulates imagination, that may be where the human need comes from."

There is a certain quality of depth in Artists who paint purely from their imagination and intuition. Pretension and concepts are stripped away, revealing human qualities and personal truths. This is perhaps quintessentially Amy, who enjoys making art, led by her 'free and uneducated will."

going by leaf

dillydally ticky-tock

Amy Sol

music of the turtles

leaving downey cloud island

the uncaging of loll spirits

land of dreams

Cabizbaja

"I realize in my paintings, there is a drive, a level of drama and melancholy."

Analog and digital techniques find a happy marriage in the work of Cabizbaja. She expresses that she is happy whenever she sees her work in print, on the web or on gallery walls. On a daily basis, she tries to find humor, beauty, magic and tenderness in life, of which she composes in her work.

Her personal philosophy is to "try and convert lower human passion and drives, into something more akin to kindness. I would like to take it to higher levels, without robbing it of its supposedly negative essence. Trying to convert angels into demons, and demons into angels."

Cabizbaja grew up and is still living in Columbia, Latin America and is a graphic designer and illustrator. As her father was a publisher, she was as a child, surrounded by canvases, cameras and instruments. Sharing his artistic sensibility with her, she grew up always involved in creative projects.

Later, she went on to study graphic design in Colegiatura Colombiana. Since she graduated, she finds time to balance her office work and illustration, which she does on a free lance basis. Her personal artworks are also something that she is constantly immersed in.

Currently, Cabizbaja is based as a graphic designer in a female clothing brand, drawing up prints and embroidery. Her personal work, on the other hand, is an impish and witty looks at personality, human interactions and relationships.

Commenting on her personal artworks, she finds that she constantly goes back to the theme of childhood.

She expresses, 'I think it is necessary to be always connected somehow to our childhood. I am trying to never let 'her' go, to always have a happy 'little' world of reference, which is properly, our destiny. That will fill us with hope in certain moments of sadness." A heightened sense of drama and melancholy, that Cabizbaja says derives from her favorite cartoons, Snoopy, Charlie Brown and friends is ever present in her offerings.

We are certain to see more of Cabizbaja's work in the future, with her in the process of creating her new website, which will be unveiled soon, filling our world with a little of her special brand of magic and tenderness.

llorona

lagrima

cigarrete

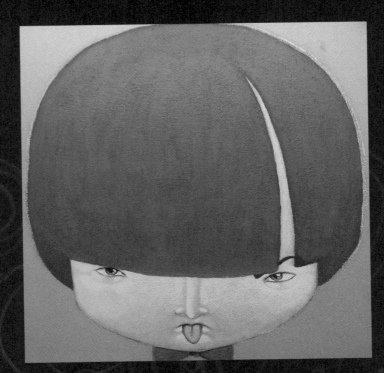

El niño

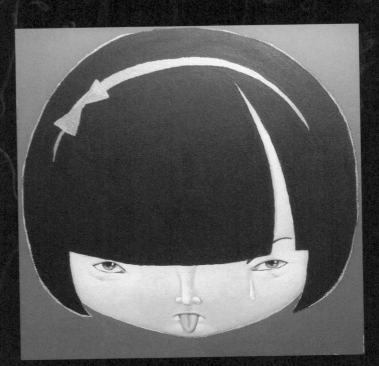

La niña

Candy Bird

I think that tales really have an initiatory role that cartoons can not give.

Candy bird is a colorful and joyful expression of things delightful and dark, represented in a 'naïve' style. This is a sharp contrast from the things that fascinate her. She is inspired by Francis Bacon, attracted to the darkness and violence that stem from his paintings. Her other favorite artists are ones whose works have a gothic tinge, such as Mark Ryden and Camille Rose Garcia.

Her imagination is the key to her illustrations. The period of childhood is of utmost importance to her. Fairytales that she knew as a child recur as visitations in her work. Intrigued by the labyrinth journey in Alice in Wonderland and the symbols that are hidden within that epic, she strives for that intensity in her creations. Chinese folk tales and stories from other countries were also devoured by this bookworm, who prefers reading to television. She says, "I think that tales really have an initiatory role that cartoons can not give."

Although her world can be 'very feminine', 'idyllic and naïve', sometimes there lurks danger in her illustrations, like a hidden wolf, poised to attack. This is a recurring

thread in most fairytales, where the characters encounter obstacles and peril they must overcome to learn life lessons.

Children, women, adorable animals and insects, like the cheerful bee that graces the front of her website are her favorite subjects.

She explains that the women in her work are her alter ego. She says, "They are very feminine, and are an ideal, a sort of perfection to me. They may seem fragile with their pale complexions, but at another glance, are mysterious and cold. They possess power."

As for her child characters, they reflect her nostalgia towards the tender years in one's life. At other times, they represent the fears and nightmares which are bound to occur during the period of childhood. Dreams that we have as children, she says, are carried on to adulthood. Toys and characters may be signifiers, of which posses values we recognize. As a result, 'we materially appropriate the artist's character to ourselves, continuing the dream."

Currently, Candybird is creating works for an upcoming art exhibition, as well as working on illustrations for a children's book, "prince and princess", creating for children what once was for her, the ultimate friend and inspiration.

sugar

daruma help me

Daniel Hyung Lim

"I got fired for sleeping in my sign making company. We needed to work on designs but spent most of the time surfing the net and falling asleep."

A large body work from Korean born, American based artist Daniel Hyung Lim are depictions of people. Whether drawing portraiture of individuals or depicting scenes of the interactions between people, the effect is charming. Cloying girls are placed in a candy coated world and saccharine colors liberally douse his images. All these add up to a certain air of romance and desire.

Although he is the first to admit that though some art is meant to be 'taken seriously', his personal works are something that he does to keep busy, and are to him, eye candy.

This is not to say that his profession is a mere hobby, for after earning his degree in Illustration, Daniel has recently moved to New York to receive his Masters in the subject. Currently, Queens is where he calls home. He reveals that his working experience include getting fired from a sign making company for falling asleep on the job.

According to Daniel, his work has evolved over the years. Where his choice in colors was once dark and muted, cheerful and light colors now weave through his paintings. He has also switched from the heavier medium of acrylic, to using color pencils.

Daniel reveals that he has a dark and depressed nature. Having gone through a traumatic period after losing his mother to depression, a change in his color palette was a natural coping mechanism.

Perhaps the light hearted subject matter of children, animals and girls serve as a much needed opposite to offset the darker aspects of human experience. After all, these are some of the things that make a world a beautiful place. The crazy colors and happy imagery that are found in Anime and Hong Kong Manga inspire Daniel. He says that their influence can be found all over his work.

Daniel has never traveled beyond the US and Korea, and hopes to see other parts of the world soon. To do this, he muses; he would need to make lots of money off his artwork. With his sweet and intense array of illustration, we are sure that his hopes will be fulfilled in the coming seasons.

sovery special

Daniel Hyung Lim

sweets

Daniel Hyung Lim

like suicide

Daniel Hyung Lim

sylviasnows

Daniel Hyung Lim

Dollydidit

In some cases, they are the anti-me. The person that I hated as a kid, or was jealous of or whatever. But even then I guess, this still reflects some aspect of myself.

JME Pool (Dollydidit) is an artist who draws from a wide variety of cultural influences. Her paintings are a mosaic of emotions, humour and personal reflections of life. A native Australian who was born and bred in Brisbane, she has been actively involved in art since high school. Her passion for learning and for art led her to Belgium for a year, where she refined her painting skills in art school, whilst absorbing the rich artistic culture and heritage of Europe.

Recently, JME visited Japan after nurturing a long time love affair with Manga and Anime, which she cites as having a huge influence on her work. Although her characters have large expressive eyes that are a strong feature of Anime characters, they

emanate a different mood, a sense of melancholia. Her characters are not all spooky and gloomy though, they possess a wicked sense of humour, and symbols of hope are a thread that runs through her work.

The process of painting for JME is a cathartic one. She says, "It is a way for me to let go of the more traumatic experiences of my childhood." She also explains, "A lot of my work is like a reflection on my childhood and growing up, and the changes that happen when you have to escape the nest and fend for yourself in the world."

Commenting on whether the people she paints are a kind of 'alter-ego', JME answers, " Yes, they are largely

a reflection of myself. Even if they are a portrait of someone else, I still put a lot of myself in them. In some cases, they are the anti-me. The person that I hated as a kid, or was jealous of or whatever. But even then I guess, this still reflects some aspect of myself."

This portraying of one's own image in art, she muses, has been a fixation of human kind from time immemorial. She cites some of the oldest art that exists are Venus Figurines and Cave paintings of hunters. She goes on to add, "I guess every one has a story to tell and we need a way to express it. For those of us that aren't so good with the words, drawing and pottery is another option."

JME Observes that human beings go through similar experiences and events, and that we all have the same needs and desires. This is perhaps why many people have commented that they identify with certain aspects of JME's works.

It is certain that JME's characters exhibit personality flaws or marks from their personal histories. They are emotionally real and honest. From the personal, yet removed standpoint of the viewer, we are given clues into our own collective histories and experiences from her images, and that is perhaps what makes her artwork so compelling.

eryn

fearful symmetry

the offering

toy soldiers

Jamie Zollars

The magic of Jamie Zollar's paintings lie in the the ability of her images to transport the viewer to a different reality, to mysterious places in far off lands. Her paintings, though possessing a certain childlike quality of naivete and innocence is however, not all sugar and spice and everything nice. Her central characters wear no masks, and the artist reveals them to be deep, dark and complex personalities. Take for example, her painting Reluctant neighbours. A girl and a bear sits uncomfortably close to each other in a cable car over looking a backdrop of moutains. Both of them are scowling, oblivious to the beauty surrounding them, caught up in their discomfort in being next to each other.

Jamie has been drawing as far back as she can remember, and since she was little, always knew she would be an artist. Her credentials boast two art degrees, one in Photography, and other in Illustration. After graduation, she joining organizations such as the Los Angeles Society of Illustrators and the Society of Children's Book Writers and Illustrators gave her a network of connections and experiences. She landed her first illustration job four years ago, and has been steadily producing an impressive body of work.

Her view on her creations, is that her 'characters' are unique. She is quick to explain that the other worlds that she paints are not an escape for her, nor her characters. What makes her characters unique are that they have their own problems. They make sacrifices, just like the rest of us, even

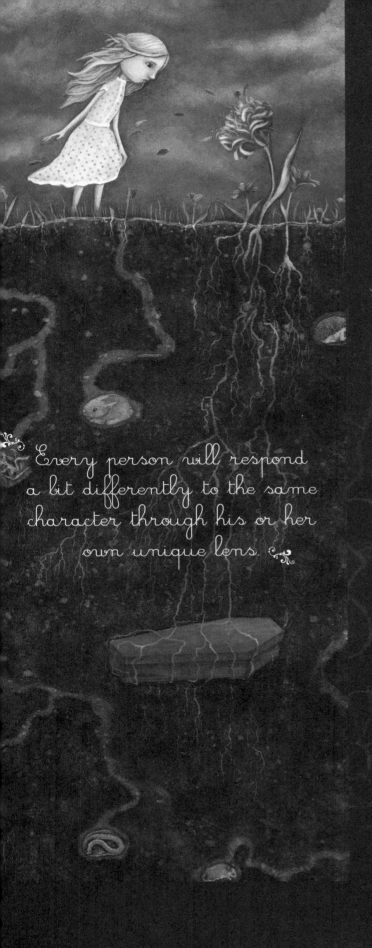

Every person will respond a bit differently to the same character through his or her own unique lens.

though they live in magical worlds. She says, "I'd love to take a trip to my candy-colored mountains or magical forests, but I know that even the characters who live there have daily struggles too." Jaime is also quick to add that her characters are not her 'alter-ego' or part of her identity, but take on a life of their own in the process of creation, living parallel lives in parallel worlds. More than being a reflection of herself, they are a reflection of the people, and the societies that make up our world.

As a child, she was most influenced by the Belgian cartoon the Smurfs, as well as the American cartoon, The Jetsons. She says, ", because their worlds were so different from my own, I could believe that worlds like these could exist somewhere far away. I think my affection for creating alternate landscapes and civilizations may have stemmed from a love of hearing and seeing childhood stories about fictional places far far away."

Jaime feels that whatever medium we immerse ourselves in, whether television, books or art, we are always relating to the characters in some form or another. "Every person will respond a bit differently to the same character through his or her own unique lens. Sometimes it is easier to explore different circumstances and emotions through the trials and tribulations of a fictional character, and these connections and subsequent realizations can be important for people." Immersing ourselves in Jaimes art, we are compelled to peel back the layers and explore the hidden depths and meanings in her images.

monster food

reluctant neighbours

oh christmas tree

Kennyswork

*Through creativity and imagination,
we can reach the worlds we want.*

Kenny of Kenny works studio is born and bred in the pearl of the orient, Hong-Kong. From his one-man studio, he presents to the world the lovable and talented Molly the painter, as well as the recently released copperhead 18 Bearbrick. Molly the painter is one of the new kids on the block, and is already proving to be an immensely popular character. With her cherubic face and golden locks, it it no wonder. She is as talented as she is good looking, and has recently had a Blythe doll made after her.

Moving from one medium to the other with ease, Kenny paints in acrylic, illustrates and is a prolific sculptor.

It was during his tender years in secondary school that his sister discovered quite by accident, that Kenny had a talent for drawing. It was with her encouragement, that he realized that this was a great love in his life, and that he wanted to pursue this. After 2 years in design school, he joined an advertising company as a visualizer. This job was grueling, but offered him solid training in terms of drawing up storyboards. The first company he set up, Studio Bee, focused on illustration. Brothers free was born in the year of 2000 where he explored his favorite medium, 3-D

figure making. Kennyswork, his solo company set up in 2006, showcases his work in all those mediums, and marks the beginning of his maturity and confidence as an artist.

Kenny's artistic vision is to bring to reality, the yearning for an ideal world, which is intrinsic to the minds of every human being. This is combined with a love of dreaming up and creating futuristic worlds and figures, which he admits, are challenging to portray. His believes however, that creativity and imagination are the pathways that lead us to the worlds that we want.

Kenny named Doraemon as one of his biggest influences, and his favourite cartoon, and revealed that Doraemon had helped him overcome many a trouble. He has nurtured a love for Japanese cartoon characters as far back as he can remember, asserting that these characters, complemented with a good story, can create deep relationships with it's audience. He believes that it is an inexplicable addiction, akin to feelings of sacredness and love.

Perhaps it is this realization of the magic and love that characters can inspire, that he unleashed his characters into the world, to brighten it up just a little.

dondelion print

molly drawing

molly the painter

clown

walking

tofu molly

Kennyswork

Kukula

The illustrations are actually a reflection of the world and life we live in via my own point of view, which is of course a very feminine point of view.

Growing up in a small town in Israel, Kukula spent her formative years engrossed in drawing ponies and princesses. The creatures that she draws today, pay homage to her childhood influences of Care Bare, My Little Pony and Holly Hobbie, as well as the 'cute little things' she began collecting since she was five. These are keepsakes of a former time which she still cherishes.

After Kukula's education in the Shenkar School of Design in Tel Aviv, with a major in illustration, she held several un-fulfilling jobs, including being a debt collector for an insurance agency. She made the big leap towards becoming an artist when she shifted to pursue her art in the USA.

Today, Kukula lives in Berkley California, where she regularly exhibits her work alongside artists such as Amy Sol and Audrey Kawasaki. She has built up a solid fan base with her imaginative and fantastical works, which she usually paints on wood, using acrylic, oils and graphite.

Kukula describes her work and figures, as molding and creating characters, after the 'ultimate woman of today, and of all ages." According to her, the woman of today is a meld of all the different types of woman of the past. Coquette, feminine, educated, independent and romantic. This collective experience of women, past and present are brought to life under Kukula's brush. It is not uncommon to see details such as a woman wearing a Victorian corset juxtaposed with Dolce and Gabanna pumps in her paintings, the fusing of clothing belonging to two very distant periods of time.

A common denominator, especially in the eyes of a character, is something that Kukula believes artists and observers are always looking for. This recognition of 'something' that is akin to our emotion, help us to relate to 'it' on a more personal level. Kukula adds that the success of anime around the world, is probably due to the clear pattern Manga artists use to express emotions their characters express. Certainly, anime has it's very own visual language.

The figures in Kukula's paintings are ethereal but strong, their eyes shine with a spectrum of human emotion, from wonder to despair to joy, a celebration and acknowledgement of the diversity of human experience.

kuku bird

from light

bru sisters

dream compass for ad

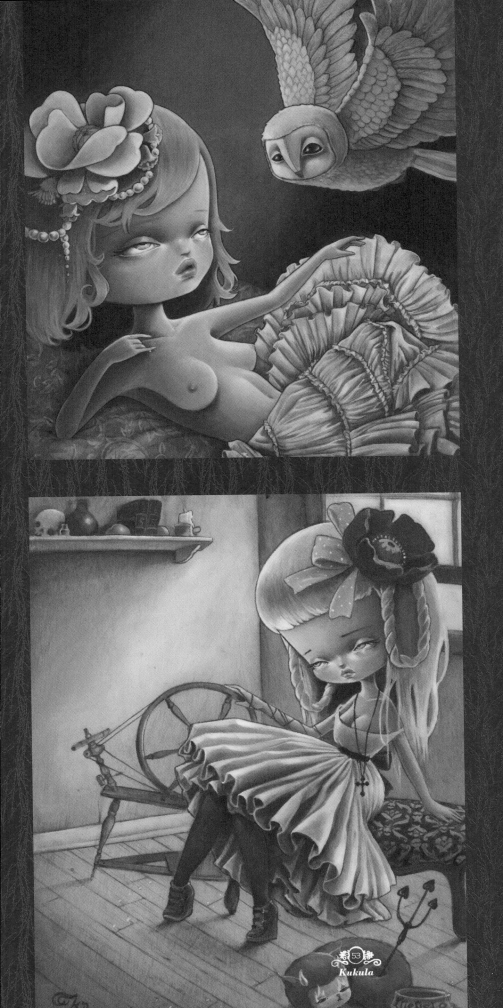

to dark

⟞⟞⟞⟩ ❦ ⟨⟝⟝⟝

faust

⟞⟞⟞⟩ ❦ ⟨⟝⟝⟝

53

Kukula

kokula pearls
med res

Imaginary characters can have all sorts of fantastic experiences and embody personality traits that we aspire to.

Lisa Petrucci takes you on a wild ride, back to the pop culture of 50's and 60's America. Her art is an array of dizzying colors, hippie-ish motifs of flowers, cute as a button kittens, naughty little girls and tantalizing femmes. Lisa extends an invitation for you to shed your inhibitions, and get up close and cozy with her art. In her world of the 'kute' and the 'karnal', extremities meet and harmonize.

What you find in her paintings is what Lisa loves in life. She is an avid collector of vintage pin ups of girls, 'when it was still a very taboo, and daring thing to do.' She also collects kitsch toys and dolls, vintage sleazy magazines of men as well as comics, influences of which, figure heavily in her work. She quips, " our house is like a pop culture emporium."

The characters that she paints are an extension of her interests, environment and obsessions. She says," Imaginary characters can have all sorts of fantastic experiences and embody personality traits that we aspire to." Getting cozy with the 'kick ass kuties' and their impish and girly characters, what emerges is a sense of exuberance, and a celebration of all that is fun and feminine. For the girls that Lisa paints exude eroticism, coupled with sass and strength. She has related that as a child, one of her role models was Wonder-woman, and that strong female characters were probably the basis of becoming who she is today.

Tracing her journey as an artist, she says that the Art that she makes today has little to do with the formal art education she has had. She relates, "Most of what I learned about painting, was from observing other artists I admired, as well as practice and experimentation, and being inspired by things that I enjoy looking at."

Certainly, her style is instantly as distinctive as it is recognizable. Lisa concedes, tongue in cheek, "Technically, the paintings are more akin to the arts and crafts hobbies of suburban housewives than the work of serious contemporary artists." Whether that is true or not, Lisa's girls have won fans in Japan, Italy and New York and is set to make more waves worldwide.

frankenkuties

little wonder woman
saves the day

bouncing bat doll

little devil

hula-la

little pirate

Mijn Schatje

If I make the things in my head concrete by drawing them, who can tell me it isn't real?

Mijn Schatje is an artist who describes her style as threading somewhere in between pop surrealism and digital lowbrow. She calls herself a 'paper dolls' maker, conjuring up images of delicate pencil lines and cut out paper. However, she says, "My one and only medium is my brain, my computer, my mouse and a classic vector software."

Her childhood was one that when told, unfolds like a fairytale. She grew up surrounded by an immensely creative family. They encouraged their children to sing, learn instruments, sculpt and draw to uncover their innate talents. Her father bought one of the first personal computers, and as a child, she spent hours learning it on her own, experimenting with the first vector art soft wares. It is no wonder that though only in her twenties, her work belies technical superiority and conveys an incredible depth and richness.

Mijn enrolled in a Fine Art school at the age of 17, which she loved, and then she went to a design school to study graphic design. Like so many an artist before her, she moved to Paris, creating personal works for pleasure. Initially she worked illustrating fashion as well as designing album covers. Eventually, Mijn met a curator. After showing him her work, he immediately offered her a show, it was an immense success and all her works were sold. That as she puts it, was how it all started.

Mijn relates that she has lived an incredible childhood, with fantastic experiences. She likens it to a fairy tale. As life today has presented her some harsher realities, she says that the only thing she can do is to keep drawing, 'to make it exist again.' She adds, "if I make the things in my head concrete by drawing them, who can tell me it isn't real?' Her work is a message to people, " that no matter how hard and sometimes ugly life can be, something else exists, in their minds."

When asked where she most likes her works to be displayed, she answered, "Some people told me that they bought my prints to display them in their childrens rooms and I think that's better than the biggest museum ever. I hope that their children will appreciate my pictures and grow up nicely, protected by my characters." One would certainly sleep better at night, with the huge dewy eyes of Mijn's dolls looking over serenely over you as you fall into slumber.

between me

licorne

dance me to the end of the world

fille montagne

fille poisson

snow white

colerette

71

Mijn Schatje

Luke Chueh

I think this current movement toward illustration is simply bringing art back to the masses.

The underground arts scene in Los Angeles has given rise to Luke Chueh, one of it's most sought after artists. Luke's art is an amalgamation of the adorable, violent and humorous, playing out in a series of tragically comical narratives.

Luke has worked hard and played his dues to emerge as one of the hottest properties of the LA arts scene and beyond. Before graduating

from Cal Poly San Luis Obispo with a BS in graphic design, he worked at the guitar and strings manufacturer Ernie Ball as a designer. In 2003, he moved to Southern California to look for work as a designer, but fortunately for us, he couldn't find any. Instead, he got immersed in the LA underground art scene and began concentrating his energies into becoming a studio artist.

Luke Holds the belief that there has 'almost always' been a major disconnection between art and it's audience. He goes on to say that before the 20th century, art was specifically made for the purpose of celebrating "God". In the 20th century, abstraction in art took art to new levels of pretentiousness. So, for him, this current movement towards illustration and illustrative styles, brings art back to the masses.

The masses have definitely reciprocated, what with the growing Low Brow art movement, and the soaring popularity and demand for more of Luke's unique works. Luke himself sums up his ethics as an artist, to find harmony and balance, between the act of "selling out" and "buying in".

Birdbrained

Possessed

Luke Chueh

> *One day I was sitting in a chair and thinking ... thinking as far as I could get. My head ached ... then I got up and decided to become an artist and go to art school. But I am not sure I learnt anything there....*

Mayo is artist, whose humor is perhaps, a tad eccentric, in a good way. Her composition is interestingly off center, while hidden elements creep up and surprise. Beetles and bugs, and half human like heads bare their teeth. Text is almost always included in her artworks, with words like "no mind games", cluing in the viewer on the mood and tone of the piece. Although the subject matter is at times despondent, i.e. half human, half-animal like creatures caught up in their own quagmires, the color and naïve illustration style offers hope that perhaps, in the bigger picture, things are not as bleak as they may seem.

Mayo adores working with traditional tools such as the brush, pencil and paint, savoring her favorite moment when she thins down the watercolors on paper. She does almost everything by hand, including making her own vintage paper. Finally though, she uses a Wacom pad for collaging and the finish.

Her favorite characters while she was young, were not cartoons, but live animals. Spending time catching frogs, climbing trees to get sweet cherries and playing with cats and dogs, were things she loved immensely. Mayo says that her childhood playmates had an intense influence on her, and is today, still visible in her art.

Mayo believes, that the three major questions that we seek answers to in life, "Where do I come from? Where am I? Where am I going?", causes us to create masks. For her, these masks are like the characters we create in order to express emotion. Mayo goes on to say that, in her view, 'rich' civilization has lost this need to find our true selves beneath the mask of 'other' characters. She says, "It is different in places where the world really isn't a fairy tale, where getting food is equally essential to breathing air. In these places, fairy tale is still about the battle between good and evil, in the CLEANEST FORM!"

It is perhaps this consciousness that informs her art, for we see the characters in sometimes lost, or overwhelmed in strange gardens and landscapes, seeking to emerge from the dark world of the chrysalis into the light.

wild flower

on the way somewhere

mayo moon

NO MIND G

no mind GAM

no mind Gar

no mind Ga

cat bird

on Freuds couch

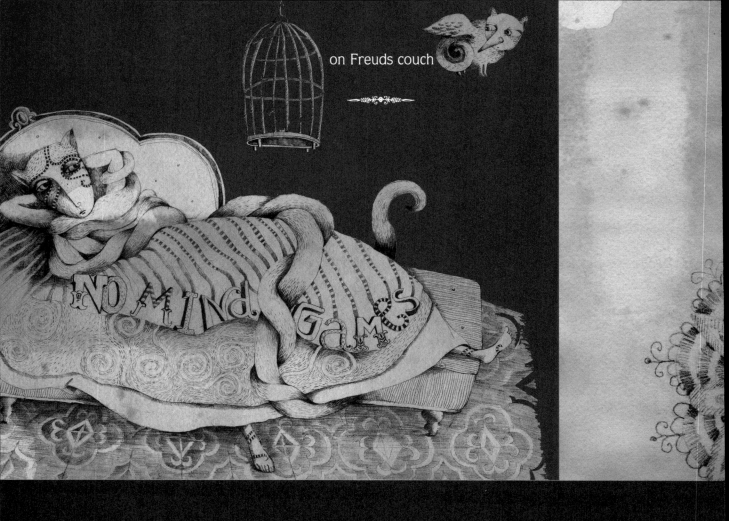

where is mayo

no mind

NO
MI
NO
GAMES

no
mind

WILD GARDEN

NO MIND GAMES no mi
no mind GAMES NO mind games
no mind Games
no mind Games
mind Ga
Games

mayo

mayo

passiflora

Passiflora

the deer hunter

Melanie Florian

I remember we were walking on the Moutain Vosges and he was telling me all these stories while we were chasing fairies!

The two most important things in the life of illustrator and artist Melanie Florian are drawing and children. Having just graduated from Art School, she is newly beginning her career as an illustrator and author for children's books.

Before Melanie went to art school, she had a strong desire to work with poor and abused children. The plight of the children in Cambodia especially spoke to her. After college at 18, she worked at a school for educators of young children. Childcare centers, hospitals and orphanages were some of the places where she put worked. At the tender age of 18, she found the work too psychologically demanding. She was also getting frustrated as she could not find time to draw. Melanie then decided to pursue the other great love in life, art.

In the June of 2007, Melanie has finally completed four years of hard work in the famous school of illustration, the "Emile Cohl" in Lyon. She comments that she has had exposure to both contemporary art in Montepellier where she dabbled in painting, making sculptures, collage and where she uncovered the 'deeply hidden parts' of herself. In Lyon, where the focus was more on technical learning, she honed her drawing skills. She says that she is lucky to have known two very different approaches to art.

As a child, Melanie's father told her stories of faeries, elves and other creatures that lived in mystical forests. One of her most vivid memories were of trekking with him on the Moutain Vosges, where she and him chased faeries. They looked for faery traces and took photos, which eventually mysteriously disappeared. The artwork that she produces today, are of children of all nationalities and ethnicities, her work has a definitely charming 'faery vibration'. These works are something she wishes to share with children. She expresses, "i wish to "help" them that way, with my stories and my drawings."

Fairytales and stories, Melanie believes, are a human need, and help us to connect with our souls. She says, "they help us to create our world, to express our feelings, they help us communicate in a different way. It's like communicating soul to soul. It's also a way to tell subtle things, to communicate soul to soul, to touch people. Stories are like parables. People need to dream."

Melanie leaves us with a beautiful thoughts and feelings with her inspiring artwork and beliefs. Art and creativity for her are a vital link with our souls, helping us open our minds, to become conscious of the vastness of the world and existence. Finally, it is a connection to our spirituality, something that takes us out of mundane daily life.

dessine

Mélanie Florian

boudeuse

calin

Melanie Florian

Nicoletta Ceccoli

*I try to find a different approach
on each project I have to illustrate*

The mysterious, lifeless beauty of antique dolls is the core inspiration for the pale and gothic beauty of Nicoletta Ceccoli's illustrations. A prolific artist, she has illustrated several children's books and has exhibited her work in Paris, Los Angeles and Osaka. In 2001, she was awarded the Andersen Prize, elected as the best Italian illustrator of the year. More recently, in 2006, she was awarded the silver medal from New York's Society of Illustrators.

Nicoletta's father was a furniture wood worker, and she spent her childhood working with her hands, fashioning toys out of wood, helped by her father. She later went to the Institute of Art in Urbino, Italy, graduating with a degree in Animation. The desire to tell her own stories through drawings was always strong, and she soon got her first jobs from publishers who saw her portfolio. Today, she has illustrated many books, published in Italy, the US and the UK.

Of her own work, she explains that she often creates settings that are 'silent' and solitary, her figures are lonely creatures who wallow in a moody and dark atmosphere she likens to 'bittersweet nightmares'. These girl figures are often 'abandoned' floating in empty spaces, while an impending sense of threat hovers near.

Nicoletta believes then when children play and come into contact with dolls and toys, they give life to their own fantasies, exorcizing fears by the act of play. She likens the process of drawing to a child playing, regressing into a world of innocence while creating.

Working with all sorts of material, from paper, pencil to computers, she sometimes models clay figures and photographs them digitally. Switching between the computer (Photoshop) and to pencil and brushes and even trying the airbrush give Nicoletta's work an authentically rustic feel.

Leading us into a world of delight and untold stories, Nicoletta unravels a threads that engages us to explore the mystery that lies under the surface of everyday living.

Nicoletta Ceccoli

flora

butterfly

treegirl

eggirl

bee dream

rosalie

sheryl

Nicoletta Ceccoli

fish & girl

tower

cowgirl

grasshopper and girl

spidergirl

coniglietta

catgirl

catgirl

Creativity and imagination are powerful tools, but they always need someone to care and nurture them. That is what characters do best.

Noferin is the creative duo comprising of Candy and Nicho,who live in Melbourne, Australia. They reveal that their real home however, is Carrara Island. Carrara island is where the pecan pals frolick under shade and sun, dreaming up new adventures and living the good life. With such marvelous friends to meet and greet, who can resist joining in?

The creators of pecan pal need an introduction. Candy is a self-taught artist with a Graphic Design background. The developing of the 'arty' side of Noferin initially started out as just a fun thing to do. Luckily for us, her friends saw that she was on to something good. With their encouragement and support, Noferin

decided to develop their special world further, to share with even more people. Since then, Candy has never looked back, and has become a full-time artist.

The other half of Noferin is Nicho, who is currently studying for an Environmental Science degree. Nicho Masterfully weaves the literary side of Noferin. This is a winning combination, for with their combined energies, every flower, tree and moutain of Carrarra Island, comes to life.

Noferin's influences stem from a cartoon diet of Disney and Miyazaki. Miyazaki they say, has created characters that remain deep in their

hearts. Something that they try to emulate from Miyazaki, is his ability to capture details of a world, that other people do not notice. The strength of personalities that his characters possess, as well as the poignant messages, is something that they try to emulate.

The relationship that human being form in their hearts to characters, they explain, "enable people to understand the world better. They serve as entities that people can identify and associate with. They can take you away on adventures, entertain you, educate and give you a feeling of safety and comfort. Most of all, they are a friend." "Creativity and imagination are

powerful tools," they add,"but they always need someone to care and nurture them. That is what characters do best."

Of course, all characters have a special home, and they are glad to have an environment of such lush and wondrous beauty. "The Australian landscape is much, much more than what people instantly think of. It is more than just beach and desert! It is a country of extremes and hidden treasures." When Noferin are not busy painting and writing, they explore their natural surroundings as often as possible, thinking and dreaming up new landscapes for their pecanpals to inhabit.

Phunk Studio

Phunk Studio

What is universal truth? We are interested to find out more by exploring the system, It has evolved to become a constant recurring theme in our works, and that recurring message is 'Love'

In a Singaporean art college in the early nineties, four individuals, drawn together by the common love for British Indie music, American pop culture, parties and Kung-Fu and Chinese mythology forged a lasting friendship. This relationship would eventually become Phunk Studio, a graphic design team that has helped put Singapore firmly on the International map of graphic design.

Phunk studio has created their own imaginary universe, which they say, "illustrates a dysfunctional tale of an apocalyptic society where good and evil co-exist. It is a world inhabited by both man and god with its own contradicting system of universal truism and values." This universality is examined in the context of the symbolic relationship an individual has with his universe, in the age of modern globalization

and technological advancement. An urban mythological tale, informed by social satire and popular culture is created, infused with Phunk Studio's unique visual language, iconography and wit.

Finding that boredom sets in quickly, Phunk Studio constantly explores different channels of communication and expression through varied mediums. This allows for the blurring of lines and boundaries, "between art and design, creative and commerce, craft and technology, east and west, control and chaos, love and hate, friendship and partnership, audio and visual. Currently, Phunk Studio is spreading their message through the medium of fine art, print, painting, sculpture, installation works in different galleries and public spaces.

creature

Brandt Peter

My paintings and visuals tend to take those past childhood memories and experiences and twist them into the worlds, characters and environments that you see today

The subject of Brandt peter's paintings stem from the 'personifications of experiences' in his life. Some of his paintings are haunting, others are surreal explorations . Some are mirrors held up to society, potraying misfits who live on the fringes, as in his series 'Intinerant Misfits.'

Brandt was brought up in Southern California, in a home that was filled with antiques, tin toys, vintage cartoons, retro advertising materials and circus/side-show paraphernalia. Growing up with creative parents who were supportive of his choice to be a visual artist, he was lead on a journey that has seen him working in diverse and different fields, from comic books, to theme park development, film as well as animation design.

Today, Brandts paintings are excecuted in the medium of oil on canvas. His series of paintings ' Slap-Happy!', are based on him as a child. The child hiding behind a skeleton mask represents his defense mechanism, one that empowers, but simultaneously yields to bravery, weakness and fragility. 'Miss Content' is a character inspired by his wife, fellow artist Kathie Olivas, creator of Misery children. As his muse and biggest inspiration, he says " she taught me to paint and showed me how to have a voice and follow it."

Explaining the ideas behind his work further, Brandt says "I believe my work speaks on many different levels, and that's why there is an instant connection and understanding from the viewer,

something they connect to, something strangely familiar... Regardless of what generation you're from, as icons they carry the same overall meaning."

The human connection that is forged with cartoon characters, comics as well as fairytales is one that Brandt identifies with. He says, "I can completely relate to these characters and worlds – On many different levels, they become stronger than words, less restricted than reality, more authentic than truth – they cross boundaries that normally language and social code get in the way of. In a way, it may also remind us of a simpler time, like when we were kids – everything we saw ... we saw for the first time – Our attitudes pure... An uncharted world filled with vast opportunities, ready

to believe. We tend to lose this when we get older... Toys, Characters, Animation become a way we hold on to our innocence."

The characters of Brandt's world are definately special,as they also serve as a commentary on society. He questions socially acceptable behaviour, and the punishment that is dished out to people who do not seemingly conform or fit in that standard. On the surface, his characters are lonely misfits and alienated personas. It is Brandt's intention to allow people to see his characters as mirrors, reflecting the reality of the ourselves beneath our personas.

Confronted, we are left to come up with our own answers.

Brandt Peter

see saw

№ 16. no 16

.A

.B

b

114

Brandt Peter

fetish girl

octopus rider

bp bearboy rabbit

rabbitboy collab

Brandt Peter

Danielle Lamberti

My paintings are defiantly the bad side of me I wish can come out.

Bimba and Pupa in Italian-speak means dolls. These are the characters of Danielle Lamberti, who was born and raised in a 'typical Italian family' in Brooklyn New York. Going to an all-girl Catholic high school, and being deeply religious, she says, "I live everyday for the next life. My paintings are defiantly the bad side of me I wish can come out." Where she has a shy and quiet nature, her girls are boisterous. Girls in the five boroughs of New York, and bad behavior are what inspire these sassy and rainbow colored paintings. Her ideal heaven, Danielle muses, will look like Willy Wonka's chocolate factory.

Strawberry shortcake, the Rainbow Brite dolls from the 80's and

Hello Kitty are Danielle's favorite characters. She says that there exist many 'Kidults' who having reached adulthood, yearn to return to the more innocent time of childhood. Admitting that she herself is one of them, she says that, "Painting brings me back to a "Kidult" state of mind. I feel like I'm 7 years old again."

There is certainly a sense of being dazzled when appreciating Danielle's Bimbas and Pupas. Hyper colors flood the senses, and to achieve this effect, she works with liquid acrylics and glitter. Glitter might be a tricky medium to apply, but when done right, as Danielle does, it looks amazing. Danielle dislikes being restricted by galleries when showing her work. She prefers displaying her

works in an installation, where she is able to create a 'whole' atmosphere. She expresses, "When you see my paintings you should feel like you yourself are in a different planet."

Before Danielle became a painter and illustrator, she harbored dreams of becoming a comic book illustrator. She went to the prestigious Pratt Institute of Brooklyn and had a short stint interning at MTV. She realized then that she wasn't crazy about the 'whole commercial world'. She interned instead, in her senior year, for the Jonathan Le Vine gallery, who specializes in showcasing 'low-brow' and pop culture infused works. A whole new world of 'new art' that was happening at the time finally captivated her, and

she dropped the idea of illustrating for children and comic books. She conveys, "I knew I had to stop listening to what was successful in the business and be true what I really wanted to draw. Which were my Bimbas and Pupas."

Sunbathing and frolicking Bimbas and Pupas, all of different nationalities that make up the multi cultural melting pot of New York, fascinate us with their delectable cheekiness. Looking deeper, however, we see, as Danielle intends, not just that these girls, "look pretty, but within the subtle icons hidden, are messages waiting to be decoded.

tats

———❖———

gluttunous

Danielle Lamberti

kitty litter

play with
my yo yo

Danielle Lamberti

sunspots

122

Danielle Lamberti

pygmy's as pets

Danielle Lamberti

Kokomoo

Maybe a little bit futilitarian.

There is a sinister edge to the work of Kokomoo. Tentacles explode out of the bellies of her girls, a woman contorts her face in pain while profusely sweating and a girl holds out a beating heart, as if offering it to the viewer. Her paintings using ink, and rendered only in black and white reminds one of Manga cartoon panels where there are a higher than usual number of mutilations and bodily violence. Her color paintings reveal a softer side, with sweet pastels, and girls testing out their super powers in a psychedelic lands.

Kokomoo, a native Chinese, moved to the capital of Beijing when she was 12. After graduating from a local University where she studied art and design, she went on to work for an advertising company as an illustrator. Eventually, she decided to develop her own style further, feeling 'boxed in' by designing to the specifications of clients. Now a freelancer, she says she is "free to concentrate on her artistic desires."

Most of the subjects that she draws, Kokomo suggests, "are about memory, games, childhood and toys." Her favorite characters are Doreamon, Black Jack as well as Pingu. In her own work, she enjoys depicting a "harsh reality in a lovely disguise." The style that is found in her work is also influenced by the 80's Chinese pop art style, which she saw everywhere while growing up.

Perhaps her philosophy in life gives us a clue to this mysterious artist, for she says that she is, " maybe a little bit futilitarian". Kokomoo says that there are so many things in this world that we don't like, will never have, and things that we don't understand. She expresses these feelings through her works. Moving away from only drawing subjects from her personal experience, she ponders and sets an encompassing theme, and creates her works around that.

The mediums that she uses vary from ink on paper, colored pencils to watercolors. The computer for her is another indispensable tool. To date, she has had several exhibitions in galleries, and in the future wants to see her work on different mediums of print such as posters, t-shirts and notebooks. These are to her are an interesting showcase, and will reach an altogether different audience.

Koralie

I think we have to adapt to the world that surrounds us while keeping a fresh approach to it, like the one of a child, and to sometimes escape through our imagination. We have to give ourselves the means to improve our reality rather than just dream.

If you are lucky enough to have been in the city of Paris, and are a graffiti aficionado, chances are you would have chanced upon one of Koralie's characters along side the famed girls of Fafi and the super furry creatures of Superkitsch. Indeed, although Koralie has had her works exhibited in and throughout galleries in France, she likes her work better when it's in the street, larger than life on the city's walls. This direct contact with the architecture gives her characters another dimension, placed within a 'real' setting. Having freed her character from the canvas square, it escapes onto the urban landscape and becomes visible to everyone.

Koralie is a dreamer, but she believes that the goals that we set for ourselves must be accessible, in order to keep motivated and optimistic. She adds that her life philosophy is, "To have dreams and to give ourselves the means to realize them, not caring about jealousy from people, and without envying the ones who succeed."

In fact, Koralie gave up her comfortable day job as an architect to pursue her passion, and is now living her life as ultra prolific artist as well as urban graffiti warrior girl.

She believes that the world, full of diversity and different cultures and traditions, is fascinating. She says, "Each people and each period have got its own clothing specificities

and rites." In her artwork, Koralie breaks these cultural boundaries, using different elements to conjure up a shy geisha in an eccentric Manga style, complete with hair styles from the French XVIII century, contrasted with Indian jewels, Iconic Russian dolls and exotic peacock feathers, a true melting pot is presented in the face of her characters. It is her hope that through looking at her artwork, people will become more open to each other, understanding and respecting the differences that make the world such an interesting place.

Shedding a different perspective on how she sees the world however, Koralie is quick to profess that this world, isn't a utopia or ideal

she just wishes was true. She is concerned that through picking up and juxtaposing 'typical elements' from different cultures, we would eventually reach a kind of patchwork uniformity, which would be a shame. Ultimately, she says, " I just seek, through my work, to show that we can create a harmony with the differences that the world proposes to us."

Koralie's social and political awareness finds its way into the life and breath of her work, infusing it with the unique color that is the globalized and multicultural societies we live in, making sense of the current world we live in, without sugar coating the sometimes less than perfect reality.

olga

KORALIE

dreamy

Koralie

peacock

PLASTIQUE
GRAFFIKTEE
KORALIE

137
Koralie

It may sound insane but it's a marvelous experience.

Marjorie Ann is making her dream a reality by enjoying life as an artist. Born and raised in Ponce, Puerto Rico, she left for the US, where she studied illustration at the Minneapolis College of Art and Design. Currently, she is illustrating her fourth Children's book, and has previously worked illustrating Christmas cards, dolls and toys, which she loves.

Striving to enchant the viewer, and to make them feel as she as an artist does, she places in her work sweet and whimsical energy that children have. Joy and innocence, which they feel readily, are also part of her work. Marjorie says that she has

the good fortune of dreaming vividly lucid dreams. In them, fantastic scenes in Technicolor unfold. She believes that she has never seen anything like them in real life, so she projects this universe through her artwork. She adds, "It may sound insane but it's a marvelous experience."

The cartoon characters that have left a lasting impact on her mind are those that have left her with feelings of sweetness and warmth in her heart. The designs, colors and visuals are just as important as their personalities. Attributes of kindness and friendliness are what attracts her, she says. In that category she includes Raggedy Ann

and Andy, Casper, Pinocchio and Bambi. Surreal characters such as The Wizard of Oz, and funny ones like the Pink Panther and Yogi bear are also amongst her favorites.

Marjorie talks about characters and archetypes. She muses about mythologies and religious beliefs producing archetypes such as heroes, villains and role models we look to as guides on our life journey. She expresses, "The art form that visually represent these new mythologies, fables, fairy tales or folk tales in a way of comic book heroes, toys, dolls, or cartoons is not different from the ancient representation made by the Greeks

and Romans in their statues of their god and heroes or the one found in Mayan temples, the stain glass of the European cathedrals or the kashina or African dolls and masks."

Majorie quotes J.K. Chesterton, "I left the fairy tale lying on the nursery floor and have not found any books so sensible since".

She leaves us with the thought, "It is possible that the truth finds its best expression in the language, both verbal and visual, of the fairy tales and the fables."

dance with grace

lullabys to clear the sky

Nina lollypop

kitty kafka in balance

robot dream

she is sorry

watching star

seastar

keep going bambinas

Mark Bodnar

Be good.

Mark Bodnar reveals a private landscape in his paintings. Seductive and strange symbolism abounds in his imagery. He describes this as, "throwing a rope to the viewer, letting them in on bits and pieces here and there." Mark says this is his way of best relating emotions and experiences, through his artwork. His philosophy to life is simple, "be good."

Currently residing in Ohio, USA, Mark has graduated from the Columbus College of Art and Design.

He works as a painter as well as an illustrator, and has been working with two friends on an animated series for the Cartoon Network that they conceived together.

This enthusiasm for cartoons has been for Mark, a life long obsession. On Saturday mornings, as early as 5 am, he would be up in the dark, with a blanket and some cereal watching Looney Tunes and Merry Melodies from the mid to late 30's. Mark says, "I was taken to some crazy world where everything

was funny. The characters, the voices, the movement, the stories… anything could happen." Since then, Mark has been sourcing out these vintage cartoons, most of which, he found out, were directed by Bob Clampett or Tex Avery. Citing the Warner Brothers, Iwerks and Fleischer Studios as being supremely entertaining, he tries to infuse that sense of spontaneity and character in their works in his own.

Currently, Mark uses Acrylic to paint on canvas, but also loves the

mediums of oil and watercolor. The galleries that he chooses to showcase his works have a 'nice, warm feeling', much like the feeling one gets while looking at his work.

To date, Mark's artwork has been shown in galleries from New York to Los Angeles and has been featured in publications such as The New York Times, and National Geographic Adventure.

m. bodnar

espectro

i might die

carry on

the hardest part

bear rug

Ryan Myer

If other people can find the same momentary amusement in what I do than the hours laboring over tiny canvases is worth it.

Ryan Myer's paintings in his own words are 'bitter – sweets'. Utilizing a candy colored palette, he paints 'sad things'. This juxtaposition of the mood of his subject matter, as opposed to the cheerful colors, are akin to listening to a Smiths song, where jangly and happy chords are offset by woeful lyrics. Ryan says, "the tiny sorrow scenes are an outlet or response to the nonsense that I and everyone deals with in everyday life in the real world."

Currently, Ryan resides about an hour north of New York City. He attended the Hartford Art School in Connecticut, and has degrees in Illustration and History. He mentions that for a lot of artist like him, who are fresh out of school, it is not a very financially rewarding profession. He has held many jobs since graduating, the most recently being a mail carrier for the US Post Office (the same job poet Charles Bukowski had).

However, Ryan says that he does not like to over complicate life. Personal happiness is of utmost importance

to him. He expresses, "There is no better way to live than going to bed content with the day."

A few recurring characters pop up in Ryan's paintings, most notably Bearboy and Bunnyboy with his beagle. These are probably the characters that most represent him. He adds that, "More than a specific character as an alter ego though, I think the deadpan emotionless expressions of the characters are me infusing myself into my paintings."

The period of the 80's whilst he was growing up, was to him 'the renaissance of the cartoon and childrens' show age.' His influences range from 'anything Pee-Wee Herman' related to Willy Wonka and the Chocolate factory. The Smurfs and He-Man, with their "flat, non-colored/non-modeled glory", hold a permanent place in his memories. Ryan believes that the 80's and 90's sub culture are a reference that is an artistic goldmine. However, his influences from these things are not stylistic, but mostly psychological. He adds, "Naughty children, truly

strange and peculiar grown ups and the palette of the 80's tend to be the foundation upon which I approach painting."

For Ryan, the artistic and creative drive is a mysterious one. He goes on to say, ". I don't want to speak for other artists, but as trivial as it may seem I like to paint things that make me laugh and if other people can find the same momentary amusement in what I do than the hours laboring over tiny canvases is worth it."

Like many artists, Ryan generally favors oil paint as a medium, but working in acrylic or gouache tends to be time-friendly, as he works by painting a lot of flat colors. To date, he has not shown his works in galleries, but the prospect of Californian galleries excite him, as they have become "almost an epicenter for this art movement." We hope that the sweet and sad Bunnyboy and Bearboy find themselves in a gallery soon.

an october elegy (opal)

peppermint snail

meager means

dispondency and the lionboy

interruption of a teddybear picnic

an unfortunate friendship

the taxidermist's daughter

ill conceived

a longing for solitude

I think that not only art influences art. Any event, person and thing that happen in your life is able to influence your feelings and to create you as individual.

Saul Zanolari's work has been described as depicting a frightening yet spiritual world. Born in Switzerland, he studied Philosophy in the University of Milan before being an artist. At the time of our interview with Saul, he had already been based in Beijing for six months, working on his next solo show at the F2 gallery. Saul has been making art since 1997, and has exhibited in art in the last two years. Since then, he has gotten attention with his unusual and original style, and has exhibited in the US, Paris, London, Milan, Tokyo, Shanghai and Beijing.

The focus of Saul's work is portraiture, and his subject matters include friends and family, as well as hybrid personalities, the features of Miss Piggy show up in his work of a drag queen. Dolls, Djs, creative and religious types also come under Saul's masterful digital manipulation. Of his work, he says, "My artworks are a reflection of the world that I'm actually living in.They talk about reality.I think that sometimes to let the brain begin it's work and to let it see something, it is necessary to show things in a different way, maybe in an unusual one."

Strangeness and then recognition are evoked in the forms that his subjects take on, projecting their own thoughts and ways of looking at the world to the viewer. Some of the images may perhaps tease and challenge the viewer with their decadence and defiance, but it is this precisely that makes Saul's work so refreshing amongst the plethora of work that is just pleasing to look at.

As for his influences, his favourite cartoons were ones where the skill and individual of the artist shone through. It is for this reason he took an especial liking to elaborate

Japanese cartoons of the eighties. He is quick to point out though, "I think that not only art influences art. Any event, person and thing that happen in your life is able to influence your feelings and to create you as individual."

For someone who had dabbled in painting and sculpture, Saul now almost exclusively exhibits his photography work. He expresses that he loves the look and feel of printing his work on glossy paper, and relishes the moment when he sees his finally translated into physicality.

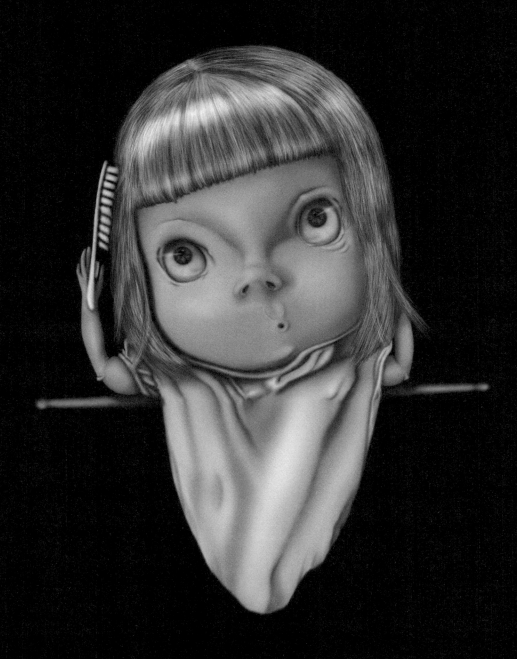

paparty book

relentlessness

chinese balls

shirley

paw

Sok Kuan

Sok Kuan

In reality, we are taught to be obedient, matured, self-controlled and so on... There are too many rules to follow and too many materialistic criteria to catch up on.

Her long black hair symbolizes "thoughts/strong will", her long eyelashes, "desire" and her deathly pale skin "innocence", meet the epitome of harmonious contradiction, Sophie Black and her creator, Malaysian illustrator Sok Kuan.

Sophie was born out of the doodling of Sok Kuan, then a frustrated graphic designer, working in a loveless day job. She found her expression and her exit from boredom in creating Sophie and her unique friends and soul mates, Owl, Crow and Black Goldfish, who keep the lonely Sophie company. Sok Kuan muses, that although Sophie may look 'evil', she is in actuality, naïve and mischievous, innocent and kind. The personality of Sophie is such that she enjoys doing things that other people find 'trivial' but she derives much pleasure from doing these 'trivial' things.

More on the creator of Sophie, Sok Kuan. She studied the art of Communication Design in Kuala Lumpur, Malaysia's One Academy. She then shifted to Singapore and worked in a small firm as a graphic designer, where she soon found herself restless. Moving to Japan for a year to study the language, she found herself exposed to a culture of many extremes and contradictions. Coming back to Singapore with a widened worldview, she worked as an art director of Ogilvy One Worldwide Singapore before embarking on dedicating herself to her personal works full time, whilst freelancing as an illustrator.

Admiring the apparent disparity and affinity of life, much like the yin and yang colors of black and white, Sok Kuan has etched out her own approach to illustration. Focusing on simplicity yet emphasizing essential details. Her virtuosity and mastery of different illustration and graphic is also a testament to her versatility and talent.

As for Sophie Black, an avatar sent out into the world in which imagination reigns and that to which we aspire, Sok Kuan has imbued her with yet another characteristic, a will to stay full of innocence, and forever young.

sophie - hair

sophie - thong

sophie - hanami

Sok Kuan

sophie in derubozu

Tim McCormick

I believe there is some kind of karmic force that keeps things in balance. With that said I know how little I really know, and that anyone who thinks they've got it all figured out it's a fool. Be fair, be honest, be patience, work hard, stay humble, throw caution to the wind.

Tim McCormick

Tim McCormick, artist and surfing aficionado was born and raised in Burbank, California. Living in Hollywood as a child was a surreal experience, for cartoons and movies were alive in everything that happened around him. Tim had the chance to watch some of his favorite shows, and other legendary shows before they were released to the general public, often in school, where the students were a test group.

In his paintings, characters loom over surreal, collage like backdrops, sometimes infused with text and hidden symbols. Tim reveals that whilst working in a construction job after dropping out from high school, the realization that he wanted to pursue fine arts suddenly hit him, seemingly out of now where.

As Tim could not afford to go to art school, he is primarily a self taught artist, Tim studied art and art history through books, art magazines and whatever else he could finds about the subject. Experimentation was a big part of the learning process, today, Tim believes that it's important for every artist to experiment with different mediums and genres. Dabbling in sculpture and collage, he says, has made him a better painter. Recently, Tim has switched to using the traditional oil on canvas, and believes that it is the best medium for painting, especially when it comes to the overall quality of the work.

Tim professes that everything that is in his paintings are fragments of a dream. Often, while painting, Tim himself feels that he is in the midst of a dream. Not questioning the origin of his images, but following an innate instinct, Tim allows the work to finish, then steps back to make concise observations about what the images mean to him. He reveals that his work is personal, ultimately, this act of painting is one that he does for himself, not for an audience.

Waxing lyrical, Tim espouses the truths that he holds dear, towards life and his artistic practice, "Be fair, be honest, be patient, work hard, stay humble, throw caution to the wind."

love letters

after all of this i've ended up here again and again

letting you into me

beautiful day

Gabrielle

Print

Adolie Day

All you need is Love

Adolie Day conjures up a serene storm with her delicate illustrations of children and animals. The softness that emanates from her pastel hued works however, not only appeal to children, but at the young at heart. French aesthetics, as well as hints of Manga and Egon Schiele can be found in her work. She cites Totoro, Hello Kitty, vintage photography and 20's fashion as her main inspirations and influences.

Other than illustrating freelance for print and showing her work in galleries, Adolie also doubles as a children's textile designer. One of her most interesting projects was painting portraits of children in her own quirky style. The likeness to her models is tangible, but interpreted as being in a delightful cartoon world.

Adolie attributes her skills to her years spent in Pivaut, an art school in Nantes, France, where she spent four years perfecting her art. Adolie believes that all artist are on a quest to find the perfect expression, and for her, illustration is the perfect way to do this. Using both traditional and modern methods, Adolie paints with acrylic and manipulates her illustrations digitally with Photoshop and illustrator. She finds satisfaction in seeing her art hung on gallery walls and on print.

At once charming and sincere, Adolie's rendering of the imaginative world in which children live in is a visually and emotionally manifestation. Quoting the Beatles to explain her life philosophy, she leaves us with a beautiful line to ponder, " All you need is Love."

Addie Day

biche

Adolie Day

sisters

pin up

Amandine Urruty

Amandine Urruty

My personal ethics, in a few words...as we say in France, trop bon trop con

French artist Amandie Urruty spent eight years in university studying art and cinema. Before becoming an illustrator, Amandine worked with huge photographs which did not satisfy her creative impulses. Finding that she quickly grew tired of the medium, she began doodling. The wonderfully strange and eccentric characters evolved out of those doodles, which gradually became increasingly detailed. Designing these characters, in the "pedantic and hackneyed style" that she favors, she tells us, " I try to utilize this kind of drawing technique to represent things like Kawai Sausages, Bling Bling, excrement and heavily breasted dolls." Bizarre details and smaller creatures densly support main characters in her illustrations.

Majority of the hosts of Amandine's characters do not possess mouths, fingers and are chronically obese. She does not offer an explanation of her character's missing body parts, although her humorous answer to the question of whether if her art is a reflection of the universe she would like to live in might shed some light. She says, " I don't think so, I will not be able to live in a world where men have no mouth to kiss me and no fingers to caress me...

Even if they can not talk about football and burp ." Also, she adds that her characters might well be considered an alter ego army but unlike her characters, she is not obese and she stresses that she does have a mouth, nose and 'ten fatty fingers."

Like many kids of her generation, Amandine used to be fond of My Little Pony. Being dwarf, nice, pink and a little chubby, she dreamt of living amongst them in their hairdressing salon until she came in contact with real ponies. Finding that they were vicious, not pink and covered with mud, she soon lost interest, turning to a harem of Barbie dolls. It is interesting then, Amandine's representation of piggy like human characters, unlike the perfectly proportioned Barbies of her childhood.

Although Amandine's characters do not possess perfect figures and model like looks, the emanate a sweetness that would melt any heart. To date, she has seen her work published in several magazines and books, on posters and had has several solo exhibitions. Parallel to her illustration activities, Amandine is currently working on a comic book entitled. "Papatte", a story about an unlucky giant poodle who looks like a meringue.

Amandine Urruty

Amandine Urruty

Memories, remorse, and fragile realities, at once gentle and cruel, sweet and unsettling.

A vulnerable sweetness exudes from the characters of Kendra Binney. Navigating or lost in a forest and exposed in the near darkness, there also exists an underlying magic, that of nature and her creatures wandering in their habitats. Executed in washes of pastel and with "candy-coated" resins, Kendra's work, " evoke both nostalgia and contempt." She says. "They are at once gentle and cruel, sweet and unsettling."

Raised in a small mountain town with no shoe stores, Kendra spent most of her time talking barefoot walks through the world of spiders, snakes and other creatures living in the grass. This is reflected in her work, where the landscapes are ethereal and dripping with a soft light. She tells us that her illustrations is a world inspired by, "memories, remorse, and fragile realities, at once gentle and cruel, sweet and unsettling."

Her lovely works have been exhibited in her native U.S, with artists such as Amy Sol, Adolie Day and Kukula. She has also collaborated with Big Cartel, in the of designing wallets, as well as featured in a book, "Invision", featuring the works of other Portland artists.

Kendra currently lives in Portland, Oregon where she paints and day dreams in her studio, dreaming up of lovely and wondrous paintings.

say

better light

let go

Kendra Binney

conquered beasts

Kendra Binney

lost homes

flew away

Kendra Binney

monsters

frail

My characters use their imagination to find some way of escaping from this harsh world, like I do with my art.

Using his characters as representatives of the people around him, Benjamin Lacombe paints to deliver his own vision of the world, and to reflect problems that he is concerned with. We see in his paintings, a girl in cage with birds hovering on the outside and in another, a tearing Saint - Bernard. Archetypal symbols are strewn about in his work, making one wonder what issues swirl about in this Artist's mind. Bejamin says. "My characters always feel themselves to be different, in the maze of society, sometimes even rejected, I feel that way too."

Certainly, in his paintings, one is reminded of Lachrymose children's classics, in the vein of one of Benjamin's favourite artists, Tim Burton. His other influences include Marc Ryden, Edward Gorey and Primitive Flemish painters.

Benjamin's art education consists of joining the Ecole Nationale des Arts Décoratifs de Paris Arts school. He dabbled in the different medias of photography, painting and video work. These days however, he cites the traditional and versatile medium of Oil paints, " for it's infinite possibility " and gouache as his favourite mediums.During his years in school, he not only interned at an animation studio in France, but diligently he worked on his first comic book series, ""L'esprit du temps" - Ed Soleil" or "The Time Spirit" at the age of 19, to pay his own way through Art school. Another editorial project that he worked on was for his school's final art project, "Olive and Cherry" which became his first Children's book. Since those formative years in school, Benjamin has kept on writing and illustrating children's

books, exhibiting his works in shows in France and The U.S. Benjamin makes known to us, " Fairy tales are a lovely way to reflect on society's problems. At the same time, they are a medium that allows us to escape from our world. Toys and characters are a persistent connection of dreams. They are maybe the only space for innocence and dreams in our pragmatic, ironic and occidental society."

Sincerity and honesty shines through in Benjamin's work, giving it quality of self revelation, as the artist himself puts it. " My characters use their imagination to find some way of escaping from this harsh world, like I do with my art."

Lacombe Benjamin

Lacombe Benjamin

Corrie Gregory

> *They opened up a world where it's safe to express ones self.*

Corrie Gregory paints animals, and hybrid animal-children in an expressive and quasi naive style. Each of her characters is replete in their own worlds, the surrounding landscapes reflecting their personal stories. She uses a variety of means to convey her interests and meaning, in some of her works, messages are coded in. "Magical thinking". "You make yourself", "Do this lesson and get well" seem to be devices and clues into the artist's inner world. Corrie favors the medium of oil and gouache, having a particular fondness for old paper. She also collects old medical books and prescriptions, some of which she uses in her mixed media works.

She says of her subject matter, "There is something about an animal or character that gives one freedom to experience emotion in a much more honest way. They are less threatening, but they still can show great darkness. It never occurred to me as a child that animals weren't capable of human emotion and thinking. These characters and images inspired me and still do. They opened up a world where it's safe to express ones self. You could disappear into this world and not have to deal with reality. I'm still exploring animals real and imagined and that's very much what I loved as a kid."

Born and raised in Los Angles CA. Corrie currently live in North Hollywood, California. Her early memories include drawing animals and people in a sketch book as well as making objects such as stuffed animals and other things on a potter's wheel. She cites the artist Max Beckham as the first she remembers who moved her, another artist she loves is Ed Kienholz, whose painting Back Seat Dodge remains as one of her favourite works of art.

Currently, Corrie divides her time between painting and working as a sign maker in a market. Her other creative pursuits include setting up an online record store with her husband. Having exhibited extensively in Los Angeles, Corrie tells us that she enjoys the exhibiting of her works as she hopes that they strike a chord in people. Her philosophy towards life is, "Be honest, work hard, and follow your heart."

little miss

casteroil

pipes - the body shop

Corrie Gregory

Corrie Gregory

Cristina Natsuko Paulos creates art in various media including painting, drawing, animation as well as installations of 'Toy Theatre.' She describes her work as, "blending themes of childhood, cultural identity, the absurdity of languages and communication with a burst of chaos and emotions."

Heavily influenced by animation styles and techniques, she breathes life and movement into her painted and drawn figures. Cristina's art is executed on a variety of rich materials such as inks, paints, dyes, craft, hand made paper, wood and mixed media.

Often in her paintings, we see two figures engaged in action, drawn out in delicate, fluid lines. Cristina tell us, "the characters I created are mirror twins of one another. They cannot exist without each other. They feed off each other." For her, the process of creating is one whereby the characters speak to her their stories, which she then brings to life. She says, "making art makes me happy. It is like a missing link. A right as humans to create and explore yourself. A quest for self-discovery. It is something I do, and I still find it a humbling thing."

Currently, Cristina works at Giant Robot NY, surrounded by cute Japanese toys all day long. A trained

Cristina Paulos

It is something I do, and I still find it a humbling thing.

animator who graduated from the California Institute of the Arts, she began immersing herself in her own art when she faced difficulty finding a job in the animation field. Today, she sees it as a blessing, as her day job fuels her artistic fire. She tells us, "I've always wanted to make art. I don't think I was ever one of those people who felt they couldn't do anything else but make art. At an early age, I was told that if you wanted to be an artist, you would end up the starving sort. And this was advice from my Mom, who coincidentally is also an artist. (the graphic design sort, not the starving variety!).I guess I've always felt that I would always have to find another means to support myself and my artistic spirit and learn to accept and be okay with that. "

Recently, Cristina has exhibited her works in The Funk House gallery in Las Vegas, and looks forward to sharing more of her stories and artwork with viewers.

Cristina Paulos

Cristina Paulos

Cristina Paulos

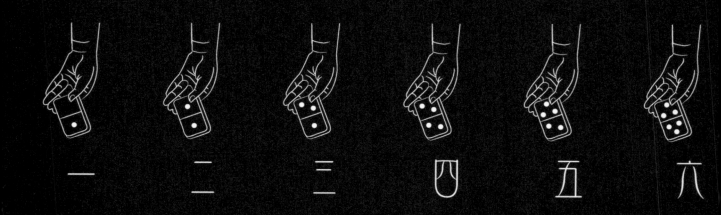

一 二 三 四 五 六

innocentgirl (andrea innocent)

Otoshimono

Some people think in words,
I like to think in pictures.

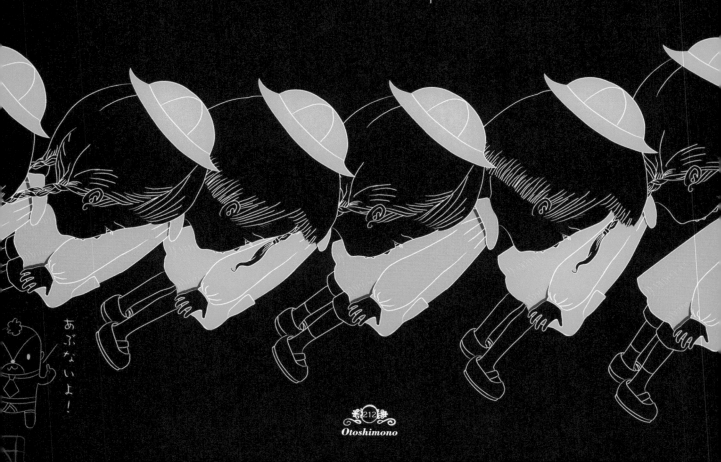

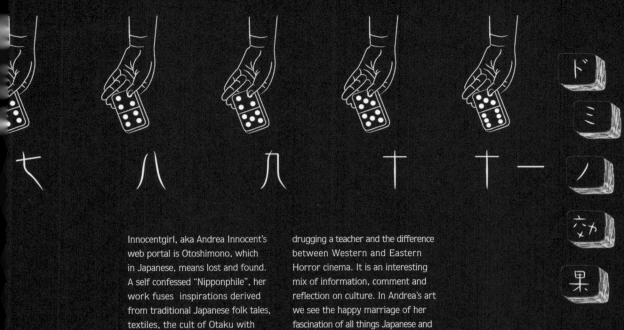

ドミノ効果

Innocentgirl, aka Andrea Innocent's web portal is Otoshimono, which in Japanese, means lost and found. A self confessed "Nipponphile", her work fuses inspirations derived from traditional Japanese folk tales, textiles, the cult of Otaku with an aesthetic leaning towards the contemporary Japanese styles of Superflat and Steampunk.

Andrea's limited edition prints such Horror Otaku, Rat Daughter, Just Be Happy etc, have a story behind them, which are explained in detail in otoshimono.org. They reflect on a variety of subjects she is interested in, such as traditional Japanese festivals, a news report on students

drugging a teacher and the difference between Western and Eastern Horror cinema. It is an interesting mix of information, comment and reflection on culture. In Andrea's art we see the happy marriage of her fascination of all things Japanese and her own Australian background.

Currently, Andrea lives in her home town Melbourne, Australia and works on CD and book covers, band posters, character , toy and web design as well as editorial illustrations. Her clients include Nylon Magazine, Calorie lab and Portland weekly. She is also always every ready for a new travelling adventure.

しゅな

ひな

futago

quickbrown

ume otaku

kaguyahime

nevada tan

rat daughter

ホラーおたく

Josh Taylor

Everyone thought he was insane, and they applauded when he was finally finished.

Josh Taylor, the mysterious creator of morose creatures and characters living in gothic and humorous situations and landscapes left the Garden of Eyecandy a note.

Josh Taylor died in the year 2037 at the young age of 57. It is still unclear the exact cause of his death, but there have been a couple of people who were close to Josh that started noticing weird things. When the autopsy was being performed, Josh was completely cut open. On the inside of his body, it was discovered that Josh had been using his innards as a canvas. While only seen by a handful of people, it has been reported that the art INSIDE of Josh is leaps and bounds greater than anything else done by anybody, anywhere. Unfortunately, the Government seized control of all works of art in the year 2012 (music was seized around 1985), so it will not be issued until the Government decides what to do with it. It is doubtful that it will ever be seen, because his art is dark and controversial. It challenges

all authority. It inspires people to question, it inspires people to seek change. One can only wonder what was created inside Josh, perhaps someday we will all be so lucky to see.

Before Josh Taylor died, however, he was born. Josh was born in a canvas in the town of Ridgewood, New Jersey. The year was 1980 and he was zero years old at the time of birth. He landed on the canvas with a loud "THUD". Josh eventually ended up at the fictional art institute called Pratt in Brooklyn, New York, where he studied Illustration and minored in something art related. He graduated at the top of his class in 2002 and was asked to speak at the graduation ceremony. Josh accepted the invitation and went on for about 25 minutes how he felt the Government was starting to get too closely involved in the art community. Josh had been drinking heavily though, so nothing was really understood. Everyone thought he was insane, and they applauded when he was finally finished.

After Josh graduated from Pratt, he moved into a tiny hermit town in Alaska and painted everyday, sending his work via DHL to his friend Todd Kurpel who was supposedly selling it to art collectors/dealers. However Todd was really selling all of Josh's art to the Government. Todd was making a fortune and only sending Josh enough cash to stay broke. More time passed and then eventually the Government passed the law claiming that They own all art work. Whether it be your child's kindergarten finger painting or Josh Taylor's "The Egyptians".

In the year 2012, when the government took over the art world, Josh lost whatever little their was left of his mind. There have been a few people to have claimed to have seen Josh swallowing his hand as far back as 2012. It's a shame really. Another tragedy. Another talented artist to never be seen. With his greatest creation trapped inside of him.

girl

Josh Taylor

tumor boy

Josh Taylor

rosie johnson

bomb boy

claire johnson

ophelia

Josh Taylor

Josh Taylor

blue namahage

Josh Taylor

dingle ghost

Juri Ueda

Juri Ueda

*I paint my images as personal letters
to the people who see them*

The pale watercolor washes of Juri Ueda's illustrations and paintings evokes the sense of a cherished girl hood, innocence, sweetness and light. Butterflies, teddy bears, flowers and heart shaped balloons are the friends and companions to bright eyed girls, dressed in their Sunday best. The influences in the work of Juri Ueda can be traced backed to the Romantic style Manga that she read as a girl, growing up in between the cities of Osaka and Bangkok. She describes her work as, "on the whole more on the other side of mainstream pop art scene in Japan today, where the cool and the stylish are the most appreciated."

Shades of her personal experience are imbued on her work, and Juri often finds that the colors, patterns and organic forms in nature inspirational, with her imagination pushing her to continually create her own world through art. In the backdrop of plant life, spiderwebs and the represented elements of air, water, fire and earth we see Juri's characters emerging, at one in their environment. We also find elements of a fairy tale romanticism in her work, for Juri tells us that she enjoyed fairy tales for their hope and magic as a kid and for their simplicity and symbolism as a grown up.

Juri stumbled upon drawing almost by accident. Before, she worked in different part time jobs as a teacher, web designer and waitress. It was during this period that she began doodling stick figures, which she found, was immensely fun. She enrolled in an art school in San Francisco and eventually graduated with a BFA in illustration.

Ultimately, for Juri, the most rewarding thing about creating art, as she says, "I paint my images as personal letters to the people who see them. It would be fantastic if anyone finds any emotional connection with my characters, or even with the colors of the world they live in."

garden flight

kitty hat

thika

calling

228

Juri Ueda

lure

wandering

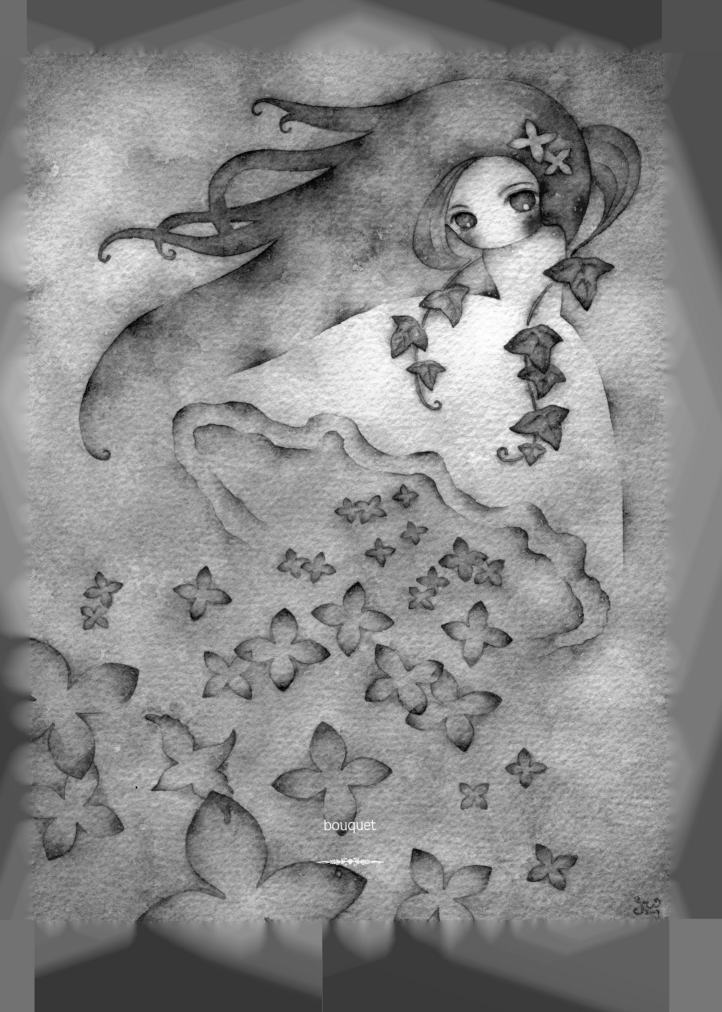

bouquet

Camilla d'Errico

Camilla d'Errico

> *The world of 2D characters is so delightful because it doesn't exist in the real world; it's a beautiful place that can be anything we imagine it to be. The laws of physics don't exist, its total escapism!*

Camilla Derrico is schooled in various different fields of the arts. Apart from having a degree in Illustration and Design, she has also studied 3D animation, in addition to having a college background in fine arts. Her passion for art began as a little girl, her time spent drawing animals and scribbling with crayons and pencils. She tells us, " I've never doubted my career path, I somehow always knew that I would find a way to be an artist in anyway that I could. I'm extremely thankful that I've been able to achieve my dreams and become a professional artist."

The world and characters that Camilla brings to life come from immersing herself deeply into her imagination, imagining the surrounding and personalities coming to life in front of her. She muses that though their lives might be more interesting than hers, she does not think she would survive if they traded places, some of the worlds she says, are "pretty intense!".

The side of her own life and herself that she allows herself to surface through art though, is through her comics. She tells us, "All of my comics are a reflection of myself. My comics allow me to tell an emotional story and in that way I can put more of myself in those characters. With each new story I create, I'm telling another side of who I am."

As a teenager, Camilla was introduced, for the first time, to Anime such as Sailor Moon and Astro Boy. She describes this as having impacted her greatly, saying, "Once I decided to go down the path of Manga, I didn't look back and embraced it as authentically as I could, its style, its characters, its stories…it changed my perspective forever. And I'm glad that it did!" She compares Anime with it's North American counterpart and finds Anime more "mature" and "moving", she muses, "They weren't necessarily silly like my previous cartoons (He-Man, She-Ra and Rainbow Brite) that always gave you a life lesson at the end of the show. Anime was on a whole other level, it was about living life.

Regarding the human connection and love for art and images, Camille says, " I think, in a way, that people can't help it, As visual creatures our eyes hunger for color, for intensity, for beauty and art is the perfect meal. The world of 2D characters is so delightful because it doesn't exist in the real world; it's a beautiful place that can be anything we imagine it to be. The laws of physics don't exist, its total escapism!" She goes on further to say, "Then a wonderful thing happens when you take those images and you give them form and shape, such as toys, we're even more fascinated by them because now they become tangible and they exist in our reality. It's really fun to have toys and figures to play with and look at and touch, its just another extension of our human curiosity."

To date, Camilla has exhibited widely in California. She says that her life's goal would be to show in Tokyo and Hong Kong. At the time writing, Camilla is achieving on of her dreams fulfilled, by exhibiting at the Taipei Toy Show in July, the first showing of her work in Asia. She will be exhibiting her new line of handbags, toys, and book Tanpopo with OSO.

feeding time

maleficent

bird buffet

cotton candy curly cue

Camilla d'Errico

red strings of fate

Camilla d'Errico

little pink ink monsters

munchie surprise

bird nest

Camilla d'Errico

Carrie Chau

Carrie Chau

The unreachable daughter, the upper hand girlfriend, the uncontrollable illustrator, unreasonable merchandiser and developer of the Wun Ying collection

Black Sheep is the latest series of works by HongKong born and bred illustrator Carrie Chau. Like the name 'black sheep' suggests, Carrie says she loves the many different compositions of herself, "the unreachable daughter, the upper hand girlfriend, the uncontrollable illustrator, unreasonable merchandiser and developer of the Wun Ying collection".

Carrie plays with the Black Sheep archetype in a humorous and light hearted manner through her potrayal of characters, cheeky and lovable, a glint of mischief shines in the eyes of their innocent faces.

Currently living and working in her native Hongkong, Carrie got involved in art in her secondary school years, where she took a ceramics course. These ceramic works became the portfolio that gave her entry in to an art and design course in a local polytechnic. She later furthered her design studies at the Kent Institute in England. She is currently lead designer for the Homeless store and has recently opened up her own store, home to her Wuying collection, which includes notebooks, clutch purses, bags, in central Hongkong.

smoke bunny

❦

pearl necklace

Carrie Chau

mid-summer

cat food

cherub

Carrie Chau

Carrie Chau

Toshiyuki Fukuda

My work gives people a happy sense of nostalgia. I try to infuse originality and mass appeal into my work at the same time.

Toshiyuki Fukuda's works possess a naive and cute appeal that is irresistible. His work spans several themes and mediums, from animals and portraits, to pixel and monotone works. The characters that appear in his illustrations are strange yet adorable, possessing their own rhythm, sparkling with vitality and life. He says, "My work gives people a happy sense of nostalgia. I try to infuse originality and mass appeal into my work at the same time."

The ability of his work to evoke a sense of nostalgia has been picked up by children story book writers, and he has collaborated on a number of children's books. Toshiyuki's illustrations have also been used for numerous Japanese publications, greeting cards, calenders, clothing, movie posters, record and CD covers as well major events.

Of his influences, he cites Mizuki Shigeru, Tsuge Yoshiharu, Yoko Tadanori and Akasegawa Genpei as his favourites.He is quick to add though, that he may have not been directly influenced by their works, but rather their thoughts and their lives.

Having a professional camera man as a father got Toshiyuki interested in commercial photography at a young age. His interest in art developed and his desire to become an illustrator was born when he was in school. Since graduating, he has worked for the illustration company Spoon Inc, as well as developing Softies and toys, in addition to his art.

Toshiyuki Fukuda

Toshiyuki Fukuda

wired

Kyung Soon Park

Illustration is a way to communicate, telling a story using a visual voice. We can have much in common with writers and storytellers.

South Korea born Kyung Soon Park's affinity with art began initially as an interest in European floral design, as she owned and ran a flower shop in Korea. When she became an International student, studying English at the Sheridan in 2000, she chanced upon an exhibition of artworks created by the faculty and students, it was love at first sight, and has never look backed since.. She took up and graduated with a Bachelors of illustration from Sheridan ITAL, and today resides in Canada and works as an illustrator.

To date, Kyung's works have been featured in several publications. She has also been awarded illustrator of the year 2007, and for putting on the best show by Creative Quarterly, (American society for illustrators).

In one of her latest works, done for the Canadian publication, Work and Life, three figures gather flowers flowing in her river, executed in a style reminiscent to water color and Ink Asian paintings, evoking the sense of poetry, peace and beauty found in village life. Kyung reveals that Ink is her favourite medium to work with, for it is, "simple and powerful, like calligraphy." Throughout her illustrations, motifs and elements of the Asian landscape, culture and identity surface. She says, "I found that artists often like to draw themselves either consciously or unconsciously. For myself, my work often reflects my own childhood. I think it is because of the transition in my life where I moved away from my childhood to a part of the world completely different than where I grew up. So somehow I include places I used to see or where I or where I would like to be but now only exist in my memories. These memories have become a big part of my imagination."

As for her characters, Kyung tells us that she tries to portray how she sees society, "When I make characters I try to portray how I see society. I illustrate people in the context of the story I am trying to tell. As an illustrator I try to expand my vision to see how other people relate to one another and how they are related to myself. Illustration is a way to communicate, telling a story using a visual voice. We can have much in common with writers and storytellers."

In her life and art, Kyung finds that growth is one of the elements that she feels strongly about. She enjoys challenging herself to make a difference in her life. She says, "It is easier to give up than change the way you think and live." She also cites having passion for what one does in life is the key to having happiness in life, as evident in her works of people doing what they love and do best.

pollution

Kyung Soon Park

frog hunting

Kyung Soon Park

birds

innocent dream

255

Kyung Soon Park

Amy Sol   www. amysol.com

———❈———

Cabizbaja   www.cabizbaja.com

———❈———

Candy Bird   www. candybird.free.fr

———❈———

Daniel Hyung Lim   www. daniel-lim.com

———❈———

Dollydidit   www. dollydidit.com

———❈———

Jamie Zollars   www. jaimezollars.com

———❈———

Kennyswork   www. kennyswork.com

———❈———

Kukula   www. kukulaland.com

———❈———

Lisa Petrucci   www. lisapetrucci.com

———❈———

Mijn Schatje   www. mijnschatje.fr

———❈———

Luke Chueh   www. lukechueh.com

———❈———

Mayo   www. mayo-nmg.com

———❈———

Melanie Florian   www. melanieflorian.canalblog.com

———❈———

Nicoletta Ceccoli   www. nicolettaceccoli.com

———❈———

Noferin   www. noferin.com

———❈———

Phunk Studio   www.phunkstudio.com

———❈———

Brandt Peters   www.brandtpeters.com

———❈———

Danielle Lamberti   www.daniellelamberti.com

———❈———

Kokomoo   www.kokomoo.com

———❈———

Koralie   www.koralie.net

Majorie Ann   www.majeakann.com

Mark Bodnar   www.markbodnar.com

Ryan Myers   www.rmyersart.com

Saul Zanolari   www.saulzanolari.com

Sok Kuan   www.sokkuan.blogspot.com

Tim Mccormick   www.timmccormickart.com

Adolie Day   www. adolieday.blogspot.com

Amandine Urruty   www. amandineurruty.free.fr

Kendra Binney   www. kendra-binney.com

Lacombe Benjamin   www.benjaminlacombe.com

Corrie Gregory   www.corriegregory.com

Cristina Paulos   www.cristinapaulos.com

Otoshimono   www.otoshimono.org

Josh Taylor   www.joshtaylorart.net

Juri Ueda   www.juriueda.com

Camilla d'Errico   www. camilladerrico.com

Carrie Chau   www.wunyingcollection.com

Toshiyuki Fukuda   www. to-fukuda.com

Kyung Soon Park   www.kparkstudio.com

GINGKO PRESS

THE GARDEN OF EYE CANDY
Copyright © 2009 by Bigbros Workshop & Basheer Graphic Books

USA / Europe Edition Published 2009 by
Gingko Press, Inc.
5768 Paradise Drive, Suite J
Corte Madera, CA 94925, USA
Tel: (415) 924-9615
Fax: (415) 924-9608
books@gingkopress.com
www.gingkopress.com

Produced by Bigbros Workshop & Basheer Graphic Books
Cover Artwork by Mijn Lchatje
Publisher I Conceptualize by I Abdul Nasser
Curator I Creative Director I Sijuan
Project Editor I Melissa Lin
Designer I Zee

ISBN 978-1-58423-312-1